NEW POEMS

*"Death Shall Have
No More Dominion'*

First Published in Australia in 2021
by Spectrum Publications Pty Ltd
a: PO Box 75, Richmond, Vic. 3121
t: (+61) 1300 540 376
f: (+61) 1300 540 737
e: spectrum@spectrumpublications.com.au
www.spectrumpublications.com.au

Design & Production by Imagine Creative
t: (+61) 1300 139 398
e: info@imaginecreative.com.au
www.imaginecreative.com.au

Front cover artwork:
The artist of the illustration, *Resurrected Irene II,* on the front cover of this publication is the W.A. artist Rose Reilly. The illustration is used with permission, the source is found at https://www.imcc.wa.edu.au/images/about-the-college/Resurrected_Irene_II_booklet.pdf

Copyright 2021 Fr Jo Dirks SSS
All rights reserved. No part of this publication may be reproduced in any manner without prior written permission of the publisher.

ISBN 978 0 86786 037 5

CONTENTS

RECENT POEMS [A]

HEXAGON	1
BLACK BERET	2
CYCLONE SECULAIRE	3
APPROACHING TRANSFORMATION	4
DREAMING THE FUTURE OF YTU	5
WRECK OF THE SIEVN VISA	6
MOSS VALE JUNCTION	7
DEATH SHALL HAVE NO MORE DOMINION	8
SCULPTURE BY THE SEA	10
HORNSBY WATER CLOCK	11
WINGED VICTORY	12
YELLOW MEGASAUR	13
THE WEDDING FEAST OF CANA	14
DREAMCATCHER	15
MATRIX OF RAIN AND FIRE	16
TERROR, TIGE	17

THE FOUR QUARTETTES

MARIAN'S RUBY JUBILEE	19
FAREWELL FRIEND	21
DAPPLED DAUGHTER	22
KURRI KURRI FIRE	23

RECENT POEMS [B]

- THE NIGHT PARROT 26
- GEOGHEGAN ARRIVES 27
- THE LYREBIRD 28
- MARIE-ANTOINETTE'S HARP 29
- THE INNER SNOWY 30
- MADE OVER CHURCH 31
- DAS INNERE KIND 32
- GOLDEN SUMMERS PAINTER 33
- IN THE YEAR 2029 34
- WALTZES WITH KANGAROOS 35
- PAUPER FUNERAL 36
- SEA BURIAL 37
- PERFORMANCE 38

THE AMERICAN SUITE

- HARD RAIN 40
- IN THE LAND OF GOD 41
- JURIDICAL TRAVAIL 43
- SOUTH WEST CHIEF I 44
- GRAND CANYON 46
- SOUTH WEST CHIEF II 48
- FROM CRYSTAL TO CHRIST 49
- OAKLAND STUNNER 51

LATEST POEMS [C]

THE MEDICAL APPOINTMENT	53
TURANGALILA	54
THE SUGAR DRAGON	55
MOUNTAIN	56
MONSTER BOMB	57
DISPELLING THE DIABOLIC	58
PAULINE MUSIC	60
THE FREE GIFT	61
BIKEFIXTATION	62
THE AVOCADO TREE	63
BRUSH WITH A BURRA	64
HOW BEAUTIFUL THE FEET	65
FAMILY SHIELD	66
MEETING OF THE COUSINS	68
KUSINETREFFEN	70
TRUE NARRATIVE	71
BLUE CAMINO	73
RUSSIAN MELODY	74
IRENE THE MARTYR	76
THE NEW SWIFT	77
UNFINISHED ALPHABET	78
WAY OF THE CROSS	79
THE CROSSING	81

BEYOND DEATH	83
BROKEN BRIDGE	84
CHRIST'S FIREBRAND	85
THE PRODIGAL'S HUT	86
THE POWER OF LOVE	87
REVISITING HARRY POTTER	88
SEA BIRTH	90
VERNACULAR CATHEDRAL	91
CARNIVAL RIDE	93
TRUE GLORY	95
I HAVE A DREAM	96
THE COLLEGE IN THE FIFTIES	97
NAMING OF BONNIE DOON	99
BAPTISM OF THE TWINS	100
ELEGIAD	101
SASHA THE BALLERINA	102
FRANK IS NINETY	103
HARING 101	104
IRISH DANTE	106
THE PARADISE TREE	107
GHOST WALK	108
ABIGAIL	110
DAMIAN THE TRAIN LOVER	112
LES AND VALERIE	113
THE CHEMO STAR-RUCK	115

BURG ROTHENFELS 116

ICE 529 AT FRANKFURT HBF 118

ICE 529 AM FRANKFURT HBF 120

NEVIGES PILGRIMAGE CHURCH 121

LOOKING BACK 122

FORGIVENESS 123

KRISTALLNACHT CANTATA.. 124

MARILYN MONROE (PRAYER FOR NORMA JEAN) 125

THE CEMETERY 127

THE VIDEO TECHNICIAN 128

WEISBACH ROMANCE 129

TRUE CLANCY 131

APPENDIX

NOTE ON THE HORNSBY WATER CLOCK 134

NEW POEMS 2016 [A]

HEXAGON

To Laurie Sullivan[1]

The mating ground of *Tyrannosaurus rex* has been found
in Colorado via the six foot rock grooves
after one hundred million years, the scientists say,
in a breathless post on the internet.
We don't have to wait that long
to discern how God works today.
The wet clay of the divine terrain
leaves a six sided imprint – two human prints and four grooves,
wheel marks made leaving the honeycomb of the Presence,
the Eucharist celebrated in love and thanksgiving.
God's folk are drawn, like bees to pollen,
and the honeycomb remains,
despite four score years and ten.

[8 May 2016]

---

[1] After breaking his hip in the sacristy at St Francis whilst vesting for Mass, Fr Laurie still presided at Mass using his four wheeled walker.

BLACK BERET
To Joseph Tro

Hoisted high by four students in a solid side-armed chair,
Honoured by dozens of Sacramentini, including the General,
Peter Nguyen Chau Hai[2] is carried up into the sanctuary
like a Jewish king, five score years old, 100 not out!
Patriarch of the Province of Martyrs, with black woollen beret,
normally silent in adoration before the Master
in the Khiet Tam chapel, embedded from France
in nineteen seventy three by Providence,
now more children than Abraham!
Deo Gratias!

[31 May 2016]

---

[2] A special Mass of thanksgiving was celebrated by dozens of Blessed Sacrament priests in the Kiet Tam Parish Church to thank God on the occasion of Fr Hai's 100th birthday.

CYCLONE SECULAIRE

The cyclone sweeps through the top end
mostly harmless, missing black and white.
What if Tracy camped above our cities,
spewing non-stop snake oil of mendacity,
a tide of cock and bull, doublespeak,
malarkey and codswallop
in a replay of the *War of the Worlds?*
This new Tracy doesn't move, unwelcome,
blasting out its counterpoint *consumo, ergo sum.*
Spend, buy, eat, drink, shop til you drop!
But more than that, every belief, every moral,
white-anted, doubted and denied.
Jesus faced this with the Sadducees:
No angel, no spirit, no resurrection.

[11 April 2016]

APPROACHING TRANSFORMATION

The car wash gets to work; high pressure squirts of water,
swirling brushes, soapy solutions, blasts of air whilst cosily cocooned,
deceived by the movement that you are moving,
whilst dead still all the time, you emerge
with a clean car but quite unchanged yourself.
Inner cleansing is of another order; letting in the light; allowing
blemishes to be seen; letting down the defences; owning
truth that can sear, wound, sterilize and heal.
The brushes and mops are still, the red light changes to green.
You move slowly forward into the light.

[24 June 2016]

DREAMING YTU'S FUTURE

Can you dream a future on demand?
Children can easily, it's a joyous game;
an adventure, entry into another land;
but adults struggle, it's a grim task, it's survival.
How many fairy tales have the hero/heroine,
cinderella/miller's daughter set a mammoth chore
with little hope? Until a benign godparent or
a rumpelstiltskin offers a dubious deal.
Coleridge's creative imagination needs to surface
our dormant gifts and free us from the bonds
that chain and shackle us to the past.
Noah believed and even patriarch Jacob worked
seven more years for his beloved Rachel.

[18 June 2016]

WRECK OF THE SIEVN VISA

'Suspected illegal exit VN' now exists;
this poet has created it; but sadly there are many such.
We're used to vessels seeking entry to Australia Felix, but try leaving
Australia on a 457 to enter England,
you will enter Kafkaland, a nightmare of bureaucracy,
a misery-go-round of forms, delays, waiting rooms
on-line or not, and bitter disappointment at the end.
Just as the Franciscan sisters of Hopkins' *Deutschland* poem were
wrecked and drowned in the Thames estuary in 1875,
exiled by the Falk Laws, so were our SSS religious
from Viet Nam in 2016 banned from the Thames
because they had no bank account! Oh ACMRO,
not Caesar's slave but gospel sandalled,
intercede for the frail and the weak!

[19 June 2016]

MOSS VALE JUNCTION

For Patrick and Mary Kearney

Twin gentle curved island platforms with blue marked letters
from A to F matching the carriages of the XPT,
generously welcoming cars to park between its platforms,
and greeting passengers with its warm waiting room
negating the southern highland chill and holding
yet one more surprise, an inner grassy courtyard quad
sheltered from the wind, haven for toddlers and seniors,
once for the Governor from his Sutton Forest manor
now cairn marked to honour a station 125 years old
by then Premier Fahey, picking up postulants for Mt Eymard
to test their vocation or returning them home again,
but not me, freshly arrived from Berry and the double mountains
of Kangaroo Valley, by-passing the contemplative sisters
of Benedictine Jamberoo, Ted Kennedy's Burrawang retreat,
and the Macquarie Pass rail line to Unanderra,
dining with Patrick and Mary on Thai cuisine, reprieved for now
from the one way journey we all must one day take.

[1 November 2016]

DEATH SHALL HAVE NO MORE DOMINION
For Michael and Michele

Naked came I out of my mother's womb …[3]
Rineke Dijkstra captures the proud mother
clad in white birthing pants standing upright
holding her newborn to her chest, one hour
after birth, hand shielding head from light;
we all make this journey, from womb,
warm, safe, pulsing, into the unknown.
Artists love to show the infant Yehoshua
in his mother's arms, cradled, held aloft,
playing blissfully with his Baptist cousin,
through school, synagogue and temple visits
to the house of the Father, learning the trade
from the carpenter abba. Then as adult
plunged into the Jordan as a public sinner,
clothed as we all are, unless born in the Amazon,
Africa or Oceania, on the road to adulthood,
challenged by Miriam to aid the bridal Cana couple,
launched on the way to the kingdom, cut off at 33,

---

[3] 'Nudus egressus sum de utero matris mei, et nudus revertar illuc, dixit Iob' (Vulgate Bible, Job 1:21); Rineke Dijkstra is a Dutch photographer who specializes in mothers and children.

laid in the tomb *and naked shall I return there* ...
but having given his life for us, we have become
his body. He lives, we live and Paul who knew him
only in the spirit, not the flesh, wrote:
death shall have no more dominion!

[15 November 2016]

SCULPTURE BY THE SEA

Before I could half say 'that is not the black fin of a giant shark …'
I knew the joke was on me; no not a shark, but for heaven's sake,
a rhinoceros, a black one, basking in the sun, belly up,
black twin horned head, and four giant trotters
perpendicular to the yellowy coarse soft sand,
sculpture one hundred titled *Buried Rhino*
spectacular inverted star of *Sculpture By The Sea*
at Tamarama Beach a cliff or two from Bondi.
Wife and husband team Gillie and Marc Schattner
star-succeed to focus on the plight of the rhino
hunted close to extinction by our trophy mind set.
As the Renaissance folk had to learn
that the earth moves round the sun
so we must let go that we are the pinnacle and apex
of the cosmos; part of it yes, but not its ego-centre:
Laudato si, mi Signore, per sor'Acqua

[7 November 2016]

THE HORNSBY WATER CLOCK[1]

Grand promise of *Man Time and Environment,*
failed deliveroo of Greek, Chinese and Anglo-Swiss
multi-kulti tech in euro zone, a multi-million
dollar cocktail babble
of bronze levers, cogs
and buckets that can't tell the time
coz of chicken bones and fast food junk.
Just for trimmings, add the trumpery of an eighteen
chime hand played carillon - imagine that!
Fountain of chaos and fantasy, topped by a sea–eagle,
primed by buddhakins, fruit bats and penguins
in reality a *clepsydra*, a water stealer,
a cunning contrivance, thieving
the public purse with undoable maintenance.
But the water remains real and the plashing sound
soothes the dry sterility of arid mall-souls,
the old are drawn to it and mothers with their toddlers.
Blessed are they in the Florence Street walk!

[9 November 2016]

WINGED VICTORY

Poised, erect, triumphant, sword down
Nike stands, no need for menace, threat or force;
gracious to friend and former foe alike
before the town hall where memories hold sway
of battles, campaigns and comrades lost.
Her proud prototype battered by age
lies unscathed in Canberra storage.
Nearby at St Brigid's, the sorrowful Virgin
cradles her son, but the goddess, wings aloft,
still on a pillar above the human travail
of Marrickville, not headless sister Samothrace,
for Darien Pullen has gifted you a human face.

[13 November 2016]

YELLOW MEGASAUR

Hooked, beaked yellow necked megasaur
no dream or nightmare monster, real giant
crawling along the ocean's edge to the gully
where the prehistoric bones were found
its steel jaws dreadful more by far
fighting nature's cascades of water
funneled into violent estuary storm run offs.

[17 November 2016]

THE WEDDING FEAST OF CANA
For Team 24

Four panels in Arcabas' polyptych but the mystery
dazzles with simplicity. Water into fine wine
and Mary at the heart of the banquet puzzle.
Waiters do as they are told; steward tastes the selection;
groom chastised for keeping the best to the last.
Brilliant pastel colours tell the tale of humanity
reconciled with God and the wedding guest
who is the unknown Lord. Flesh no longer opposed to spirit,
sex blessed and joined in Christ, human and divine,
in-hearted and concorded as intended
by the hands of the Creator Artist.
High on the Salette Alp stand
the ski slopes and corniches crowned
by the basilica's rainbow burst quadritych.

[18 December 2016]

DREAM-CATCHER

How do you make a poem? How do you grasp
and hold what is not tangible? How do you seize
a moonbeam? How do capture a dream? Brian Doyle[4]
captures stories, all I want is to anchor a mood,
moment, perfume, blossom.

[23 November 2016]

---

[4] Former editor of the Catholic Leader

THE MATRIX OF RAIN AND FIRE
To the women artists of Wadeye

Shimmering red against the bright blue sky
in the Bicentenary year I walked under the fierce sun
around the Rock, the national icon of the desert heart
only rivalled by the Bennelong Opera House
enjoying its shadows, crevices and hidden pools
but now Uluru comes Christmas gift wrapped deep violet,
a fantastic dessert sauced with white brulée streaming
down every crack, ledge, chimney, gully, face, arête and buttress
as spray, bridal veils, rivulets, streams, twin, triple and storied falls,
gushing torrents, wild cascades, thundrous roarings
dozens, dozens of them, not one the same, none identical
but each unique and individual, forming a mobile filigree
of silver spending itself in profligate abundance.
Once I overflew at sunset and saw the blazing
incandescence of the fire kissed rock,
brighter than burning gold, wondrous in the gloom.

[27 December 2016]

TERROR, TIGE

In memory of Peter Auty

Terror is a word I learnt from Peter; a blight
of the spirit, choker of life and worse, sheer fear.
The French Revolution had its Terror, meant
to protect and preserve the rights of man,
in the face of sensuality, sloth, pride and lucre
but in reality taking the *droits humaines* away.
Robespierre, the incorruptible guardian of the Republic,
often called priest, monk, zealot and prophet of the poor,
applied the law with the guillotine to purify politics
much as in the Church mortal sin once dominated
every waking and quaking fearful moment.
Is man then a wolf to man? Is Blake's tiger, red in tooth
and claw, our true nature? Do roses grow out of night soil?
Self awareness is prime; know thyself, said Socrates,
or the oracle at the temple of Apollo at Delphi?
Far better the invitation of Jesus, Come and see.
The bush bard with his pithy phrases might agree.

[29 December 2016]

THE FOUR QUARTETTES

MARIAN'S RUBY JUBILEE
To Marian McClelland SSS

Sitting on the bench seat gazing across to Mornington harbour,
bobbing with boats in the lee of the damaged breakwater
wondering if it were legal to be here as the cliff path
has been closed all year. The doves coo, the waves wash
the sand far below; a cricket sings, a gentle breeze blows
and the golden staircase to heaven becomes more defined.
A cliff track walker says: *You have picked the best spot!*
In less than two days' time Marian will celebrate her jubilee.
I will make her a poem. Have forty years really gone?
Those splendid festive suppers at Hampden Road!
Where are Betty, Maureen, Charito and Carol now
and Peter Julian, Joan and Elizabeth? You too had
a beach place near the Hotel Dava on the Esplanade;
the house at Newtown and the pine floor chapel,
then Marrickville, and the elegant St Michael monstrance
in the Armadale alcove worship space, the Emmaus meals
with you and Vianney at Kirrawee. Marie showed me
your new rule of life, impressive! Oh yes, the walk is legal,
the lady mayor cut the track ribbon four days before Christmas;
the scraggy eroded gully replaced by a groomed ski run.

Forty golden summers gone, blessed are you for the years
as chaplain at Kincoppel and Rose Bay and will be evermore.
Did Sr Julia send you greetings from Viet Nam? You have mine!

[1 January 2017]

FAREWELL FRIEND

In memory of Janette Gray RSM

Farewell friend Jan, you have left us far too soon!
Fond memories remain, articulated and in focus
from our 2002 Chapter where you shone light
on our diminishment with a bold musical metaphor,
Schubert's *Death and the Maiden*, both exquisite
and poignant. You reversed the order, putting first
death's honeyed words, then the maid's reply,
No, not yet. Twice I asked to borrow your robes
to wear in an academic parade to Federation Square,
twice you graciously assented. You took me by surprise
when you said, *Keep them, I won't need them anymore.*
You were now with a Cambridge PhD on the great
M-D Chenu, master of *resourcement*, regent at *Le Saulchoir*,
his *Une Ecole de Theologie* indexed in 1942; championing
post-Vatican II theology, co-founding *Concilium*, one of the giants
of the Council not to receive a red hat. What remains?
The primacy of incarnation: *humanization of any kind
becomes the suitable place for divinization.* Oh yes, we humans,
informed by God's Word, are now the lyre and the zither,
making the music of the Holy Spirit joyously resounding
throughout our galaxy, cosmos and beyond.

[2 January 2017]

DAPPLED DAUGHTER
For Jennifer Sanders RSJ

Dappled daughter of our sainted Mary MacKillop
and scholar Julian Tenison Woods,
gracious, kind hostess at Mt Eliza,
for our retreats and chapters,
close to Pelican Point where the *Weeroona*
foundered and sank with fifteen players lost
that dark night of 1892.
Now living in your sky-scraping bush hut,
Somerset, back of *Little Bourkling*,
nurturing the seekers and the searchers
on their pilgrim quest and way,
gazing at the presence
in loving contemplation,
singing songs of praise,
proclaiming God's word
and spinning bonds of love,
like the lady Julian. Hold fast to the end,
and may the bells of Norwich ring:
love, like the yellow daffodil,
is coming through the snow
for all shall be well again.
[28 January 2017]

KURRI KURRI FIRE
For Carmel Pilcher RSJ

Black, billowing, mushrooming clouds
of smoke, wild and crazy, embers
somersaulting the expressway,
crackling, roaring, sucking air,
denying oxygen and life,
attacking lungs, stifling breath
soiling all, presaging death at Kurri Kurri,
to you and your AAL trapped companions,
vain vacuation to *a place of greater safety*
for thirty RFS crews is some fire.
A man arrested on what charge?
Burnt Norton almost under the southern skies,
close holocaust, *footfalls echo in the memory,*
options taken and not taken,
The black cloud carries the sun away,
St John of the Cross: burning wood
becomes fire. Dare we imagine
our frailty consumed, becoming divine?
Desire and yearning, transformed
flesh into the *mysterion* whereof

sense fails and cannot speak,
the smoking ceremony is complete.

[24 January 2017]

RECENT POEMS [B] 2017

THE NIGHT PARROT

Spiny spinifex *triodia* is nasty to city folk and predators
but friendly to the night parrot, *pezoporus occidentalis*[5],
the most elusive and mysterious of birds, hiding
in the shelter of long silica tips, providing seed,
spears and smoke for the Australian Aborigines.
The small green ground nester is prey to feral cats
lurking near water holes, only risking safety
when temperatures hit forty degrees Celsius
and diet can't keep you cool anymore.
Four years ago, like rediscovered Tassie Tigers,
a small green flock in Pullen Pullen reserve
in SW Queensland, enjoys a nightly drink.
Bush Heritage Australia will improve the habitat
and vanish the killers. This wondrous find counts as:
'*The bird watching equivalent of finding Elvis flipping burgers
in an outback roadhouse*[6] and '*one of the holy grails,
... of the world's rarest species ...* '[7].

[5 January 2017]

---

[5] http://www.abc.net.au/news/2016-11-24/first-fledgling-night-parrot-spotted-by-researchers-since-2013/8051808
[6] Sean Dooley of Birdlife Magazine, BirdLife Australia, National Office, 60 Leicester Street, Carlton VIC 3053
[7] South Australian Museum collection manager Philippa Horton

GEOGHEGAN ARRIVES

Patrick Geoghegan left St Francis five times,
site-buyer, stone-layer and church builder,
resigning from stress in 'forty two,
mandate ended departing for Sydney in 'forty six,
moving to Geelong as Vicar General in forty eight,
sailing for Europe to recruit priests in 'forty nine,
consecrated bishop for Adelaide in 'fifty nine,
in St Francis Cathedral by Polding and Wilson.
Now he arrives to stay once and for all, courtesy
of Darien Pullen, portly, dapper, happy
welcoming presence for all. Friend of the poor,
orphan himself, peace-maker who nearly died
in sectarian gun fire in Queen Street;
bronzed Aussie hero, here, not over there
in Dublin, where he was born and where he died
from throat cancer. Now he preaches day and night.

[5 January 2017]

THE LYREBIRD
For Laura Kretiuk

The chief song bird is *menura superba,*
cool rain-forest dweller, trilling half day long,
Shakespeare of the bush, earth's greatest mime
of callings: dingoes yowling, kookaburras laughing,
magpies caroling, forming sonnets sweeter
than blackbird, nightingale and tweet-evers,
world's first swoon-singer, rhymer,
pitch maestro and voice supremo,
copying human sounds too: mill whistle, buzzing saws,
'larms, mokes, rifle-cracks, cam clicks, wailing infants,
mobile ding dongs, human babblings. You can hear the song
a mile away, it does not die, remembered, is sung
after death, song immortal, singer sadly mortal.
I spied you singing and dancing below the snow
in the dank woodlands of Mt Erica. Did Olivier
Messiaen ever catch you compose? Yes, in *The Lyrebird
and The Bride-City,* third movement of *Illuminations
of the Beyond,* completed just before his death[8].
[6 January 2017]

---

[8] http://hdl.handle.net/1959.14/1058015

MARIE-ANTOINETTE'S HARP
To all scapegoats

Born in the Hofburg by the Danube,
youngest daughter of Francis I and Maria-Theresa,
sister to Carolina, Amalia, Christina, Anna, Josepha,
Elisabeth, Joanna and Carolina II;
meeting Amadeus himself, both aged seven,
playing flute, harp and harpsichord, morphing into
Marie-Antoinette, young, blonde and beautiful, proxy promised
in Vienna, aged fifteen to the Sun King heir, wed at Versailles,
gifted France three children, interned at Tuileries and Temple,
scapegoated, cropped and shorn, drawn by open charette,
no mercy carriage, to the Place de la revolution,
leaving behind your golden harp
and unplayed melodies, forever doomed in Paris,
dead at thirty seven; forlorn music unheard
in the southern hemisphere, where La Perouse,
despatched by your Louis, sailed unknown deeps
to *terra incognita* and perished. *Let them eat brioche*,
a Rousseau quote, before Maria-Antonia came to France,
in the NGA café, debating theories of Réné Girard.
[15 January 2017]

THE INNER SNOWY

To John Pugh SSS and Nicholas Cowall

Once I wrote reflections on the Snowy[9],
Australia's most iconic river, poor words
falling and swirling for true passage.
Between the Hydro and the Snowy
nestle Gunningrah Transfiguration Monastery
and Bungarby Presentation Convent,
west-wild of the Monaro High Plains,
Russian formatted in native hardwood,
with Abbot Sergius and Abbess Anna leading
their flocks, house church sustained
through honey-hives, needle-work and rainbow pots.
The Snowy River marks their borders,
and feeds the shallows, deeps,
rough boulders and silent pools
of the human heart, for what upholds the spirit
is the peerless beauty of their holy icons
showing the serene mystery, not set in time,
but in the eternal now, the divine outreach.
[29 January 2017]

---

[9] Inner Snowy. Spectrum Publications, 1981

MADE-OVER CHURCH

Climbing the same six stone steps of the red brick
church as a pre-teen, but now a senior, surprised
to feel the spongy carpet underfoot and the cool air-con
where once I heard the Irish PP bawl out some
hapless penitent in the confessional. The magi still adore
the new born babe in the four gothic windows
above the altar. The unchasubled priest three times
comes down to the wheelchaired woman to lay hands,
anoint and give communion, switching to Italian
as is meet. I sit on the comfy padded cushion,
glance at the bi-lingual pew sheet of today's Readings
and admire the lovely Mimovich Mary in the garden
as I leave.

[4 February 2017]

DAS INNERE KIND

Für Peter Allemeier

Schöne Sommerabend im Myer Music Bowl
in Melbourne, keine dünne Mode-Heidi, schmunzelnd,
lieb und freundlich, üppig, lang-haarig
in schwarzes Kleid, mütterliches Elena
Kats Chernin tritt oder hüpfte auf die Bühne,
strahlend begrüsst sie uns alle.
Was folgt mit ihr Musik, *Golden Kitsch*
war frohlockende Freude, Freude nicht aus Eliseum,
sondern aus Spielklavier, Rakatak, Timpani,
Glockenspiel und Tamburin, und die MSO
Herrschaften müssten singen:
"Jingle, Jingle, Jingle".
Das war was!

[12 February 2017]

GOLDEN SUMMERS PAINTER
For Margaret Benney

The red Bell Street bus labours round the cemetery hill
then roars past the Austin to the Heidelberg shops.
I climb steep Cape Street to St John's church and school
where the bullies' battleground awaited, now morphed
into a quaint labyrinth of spiritual memorial,
crossed once for all to Mercy College where the great
wall of Strine melted and dissolved in three weeks,
reconciled and companioned before '49's end,
caught in the first communion photo, not to meet again
until the OLMC Centenary Mass and your Ovens River
art, the Golden Summers I loved. Your opal pearls
of curling creeks and misty mountains illumine my room,
You, beloved wife of Jack, loved mother and gran,
mellowing under a straw hat in the sun of Craigieburn.

[10 March 2017]

IN THE YEAR 2029

David took a census of young men of military age
and knew he had overstepped the mark when the prophet
had him choose twixt years of famine, months of war or days of plague,
so the people suffered pestilence and perished in thousands.
How dare we look into the future? We do not live
on bread alone, by the pundits, bloggers, critics, savants,
social scientists and statisticians graphing what will be,
but our every breath is God-given, widows' sacrifices offered,
risks by the young dared. What is the final outcome
in this roulette of roads taken and not taken?
Are we to be a minority employing one percent
of the population? That is already the case! Are we to be
a Filipino-VN church, again we're well on the way?
What has happened to the way we were? Ageing, death
and the withheld committal of the young,
blighted and scandalized for generations to their children's children
by the unhealed wounds of sexual abuse.
Will there be a centenary celebration for the Australian SSS
in Melbourne Town Hall as in 2004?
[6 May 2017]

WALTZES WITH KANGAROOS
For Sajeewa De Silva SSS

US Civil War hero John Dunbar asked for a post
far from the madding slaughter of battle
in the vast grassy plains of the mid-west
with only his horse and a curious white socks wolf
for company until he met the folk who gave him
a new name *'Dances with Wolves'*.
You, Sajeewa, have come from steamy Sri Lanka
to our grass castles. Within three days you have visited our aged
and asked for transport access to them, the Royal Park Zoo,
where both iron horses will let you on and off
close to our two legged national icon with its thumping tail.
Welcome to Australia *'Waltzes with Kangaroos'!*

[9 May 2017]

PAUPER FUNERAL
For Pat Hamilton

Funerals ought to celebrate loved ones
sing the deeds, list the virtues, praise
the many good things of a life well lived;
laugh at the foibles, enjoy the jokes,
delight in some humour, savour the memories.
But this? Eight children born to eight men,
and none present, neither the men, nor the children.
This is a poverty I had never known,
nor wish to know. Yes, I wept at the cemetery
for once met Jan, fragile flower, one OD too many,
and was comforted by her two relatives,
outnumbered by the diggers and the Vinnies
doing their charitable work
at the unmarked Rookwood plot.

[26 May 2017]

SEA BURIAL

The *Ellinis* set out from Southhampton
for Rotterdam and there the Swedes and French
boarded for the fateful voyage to Sydney.
From winter to summer in a few short days
via shock pitch, roll and heave in the Bay of Biscay,
most were sick, myself included, after the Canary Islands stop
the voyage was calm but the weather sultry. Poor Philippe,
whom I had interviewed the day before
with young wife and child, emigrating to Australia
seeking a new life as a photographer, Paris *emeritus,*
is undone by deck tennis in the tropics,
sick bay morphing into morgue; never have I seen
so many young French men crying
as we gathered shipstern at midnight,
engines thundering and quaking beneath our feet
and speech impossible in the howling wind,
after struggling through a French liturgy from
a borrowed missal and through narrow corridors
to the shrouded form readied for dispatch.
[26 May 2017]

PERFORMANCE

Artists prize performance, musicians absolutely;
but when it comes to vision battle lines are blurred.
Time, space, body, relationship between performer and audience.
Magritte fought his peers. Like Plato he separated
the here and now from its depiction. *'This is not a pipe'*
reads the caption under his painting in his own hand.
What to make of Marcel Marceau? Art yes, performance
also, then came Gilbert and George's living and singing sculptures.
But what of the radical feminists with their liberation agenda?
Even their sisters said, 'Get dressed and then start painting'.
I prized the performative utterance philosophers,
John Langshaw Austen and his ilk:
'With this ring I thee wed'. No ambiguity there.

[1 June 2017]

THE AMERICAN SUITE

HARD RAIN

For Pat Drummond

Dylan nearly lost 8 million kronas. Cash doesn't count
when you're knock knock knockin' on heaven's door
coz Bob hadn't given a talk to the good folks in Stockholm.
Songs move people. They're neither meaning nor lit.
Sung not spoken. Buddy Holly and Leadbelly
did the music heavy lifting; *Moby Dick*, *All Quiet
on the Western Front* and *The Odyssey*
are a few of the Tambourine Man's favourite things.
That's deep stuff, you're not in control with wild water,
whales and war, if a vengeful Neptune
is after your hide. Odysseus' cunning
led to Troy's doom in a ten year tussle.
Yes, a hard rain's a-gonna fall
the times have been a'changin'.

[5 June 2017]

IN THE LAND OF GOD
For the 2017 Capitulars

What does it mean to live in God's land?
Driven out by the seraphs how return to the garden
when the fiery swords bar entrance?
Promised land flowing with milk and honey,
guarded by giants – nightmare or dream?
We live so much in our doing, not being.
Eymard wrestled in the Rome retreat:
Into your hands, I commend my spirit.
Acclimatized to God, a new world emerges,
fogs vanish at the divine call to *eat and drink*
the self is given away, hardest act of all
not the sociology, psychology, theology
of love, but opening my door to Christ
with widow's-mite-union with him
into total abandonment … no other hope,
being to Christ what he was to God,
gift of self making mission fruitful …
nuptial life with the Lord, no other relationship,
to be the cardiologists at the heart of the Church,

as Frank Little[10] said at renovation time:
we were the sacramental heart
of his Archdiocese. Did Paul not ask:
what artist does not speak of his art?

[13 June 2017]

---

[10] Sir Frank Little was Archbishop of Melbourne (1974 -1996) and Patron of the 150th St Francis Restoration Appeal.

JURIDICAL TRAVAIL

The Great Wall of China parades its statutes
and prides itself in keeping out the barbarians,
but aren't we those desperadoes? We groan and sigh
at the formulations and reformulations as the wall
marches up and down the land of our horizons,
tweaked by the mandarins of the imperial court.
With the Holy Eucharist, all is heaven; without, a hell;
with Jesus's gift all is well, without gall and loss;
with God's bread, life is gala and fiesta,
without - stumbling into gloom, castling with sand.
Eymard, after Paul, sought to warn us of this: *It is
no longer I who live, but Jesus Christ who lives in me.*

[14 June 2017]

SOUTH WEST CHIEF I
For Tony Schueller SSS

Bonneted and aproned, bearded and straw-hatted,
the Amish, time outed, are betrayed by their startled eyes,
in the cavernous temple of Chicago Union station
to journey south for medical care,
cash paying, no direct bank debit or transfers.
Four linked locos east-hauling two deck flatcars
each few minutes, out-grunting our paired locos
westwarding ten two storey cars.
Historic forts line the tracks, giant
wind turbines and solar panels fly by
but not as many as in Europe.
The klaxon sounds long and mournful,
repeatedly as we approach a level crossing.
Longhorns on plains, beavers in streams,
slow crawl to a pass higher than Kosciusko,
then down to Raton, where one train shopper
got left behind with scout troops, knapsacks
in front and mountainous backpacks behind
for an eighty mile, eleven day hike plus food drops.
We meet the Sante Fe and Cimarron trails,

THE AMERICAN SUITE

wagon train country; we hear the NPS guides tell
of Commanches and battles on Green Horn Mountain,
lost by a reckless young chief, riding into gunfire.
We feel the pelts of bison and badger, see
the old T.B. clinic that once sold cold, dry air,
and limp to Grand Canyon land after sundown
because of new trackwork. The Amish disembark
the South West Chief at Albuquerque with their pilgrim packs.
Joey and his grandma got out there but not before the nine year old
gave Peggy the conductor two big hugs, *I will miss you.*
The thirsty loco drinks deeply for the next long haul
as the vendors display their ponchos and jewels.

[25 June 2017]

GRAND CANYON

Andrea from Argentina bounced into the foyer,
pony tail emerging from the red baseball cap.
I had seen the *Grand Venture* logo on the side of the mini-bus.
Energetic enthusiasm and right on time
taking seven from five continents on tour.
We are really going to the Grand Canyon,
a library of geology, scriptures guarded by the Navajo.
After one more pick-up we were on the interstate.
It was warm and Andrea wanted us in the dining hall
before the coaches and trains arrived. She succeeded,
we are first to boggle at the tiny emerald green of the
Colorado river, surviving in oceans of rock; eyed the switchbacks
down and up, gaped at the vastness of it all.
The elk grazed unconcerned in the open forest
near the south rim. We saw dozens of donkeys
in corrals not one has had a fall in a hundred years.
But seven hundred members of *homo insapiens*
fall each year by carelessness or design.
Via the Watchtower, Cameron's Trading Post saw us
scribing a circle and acknowledging the tallest mountain

in Arizona, majestic Mt St Francis with ten
snowdrifts on its summer slopes.

[26 June 2017]

SOUTH WEST CHIEF II

What a morning! The Chief thundered in at 2.30 am
four and a half hours late, we were told informally,
halted by a mudslide, as we slept on wooden benches
in Flagstaff station waiting room, lots of Latinos.
We passed a hobo sleeping trackside.
Straight to bed I slept well if short.
But in the diner, a refined Dolly Parton,
uttered a silent grace on sitting down,
chatting about her 40 delinquent boys on a farm
near Seattle, a pastor's wife, and the challenge
of loving those who had never experienced love.
And the young Hispanic fresher who has been on trains
for five days from New York before starting business
studies in Washington. Lots of desert with its sandy palette.
Down, down to the Pacific coast in wide bends,
skies all blue and earth all treeless. The interstate comes
and goes. We pass a wayside shrine, white cross and
wooden seat. On the flats the palm trees appear,
diesel locos stabled for the tough haul back up
to Arizona, now the first of the flyovers at Riverside.

[27 June 2017]

FROM CRYSTAL TO CHRIST
For Neil Austin SSS & Tony Schueller SSS

Anaheim, home of Ana, maybe grandma
Anne, the grandest in all history, her daughter
laughing as she looks to her happy husband,
the joyous child seated on her lap as the donkey
carries them both plus wineskin, the tools, the axe
and the pick. We can thank Dr Schuller, *If you can dream it,
you can do it!*, who lies interred now
next his Crystal Cathedral refusing
the university offer for the Orange bishop.
The cultural center displays
the biblical tabernacle, a tree of life,
bejewelled with scenes from Cana,
the groom with out of time bow-tie,
the shepherds adoring the babe,
Thomas before the open side, Magdalen
at the empty tomb, all by a wounded artist;
but already the sculptures anticipate what will come,
Jesus pardoning the sinful woman, covering her feet,
as stones clatter, laughing with children
and the boy with the two loaves; hooded, walking

on water. The prodigal father embraces
a tattered son; trilingual St Callistus parish is upgraded,
and the Tower of Hope lives on before 2018.[11]

[28 June 2017]

---

[11] As I wrote this poem in the Salinas Valley, the news broke that Cardinal George Pell has been charged with various offences against minors and has to appear in a Melbourne court on 18 July.

OAKLAND STUNNER[10]

Down Broadway on the free shuttle
with the Blacks and the Hispanics
to the marvel on Lake Merritt landed
pristine pure silver almond spacecraft
with its long ramp enabling direct entry
through open doors past the water portal
where Christ in hologram majesty welcomes,
as once in Chartres, but also in his tent
tabernacle, domestic and intimate.
The twelve are present and Mary also,
flanked by side pods of devotion.
The light illumines the mausoleum below
altar sourced nuclear fusion power core
transforming the anointing slab body
for resurrection. The Oakland pastor
and people are blessed indeed as they reach
for *Breaking Bread* each Sunday

[30 June 2017]

---

[12] The Cathedral of Christ the Light, opened in 2014, is in Oakland City across San Francisco Bay from San Francisco, not far from Silicon Valley.

LATEST POEMS [C]
2017 - 2021

THE MEDICAL APPOINTMENT

The figures lay on my desk for a week; at the visit
the doctor said simply: *You have diabetes.* No, I said
to myself, or if it is so, I will reverse it by hard work
and diet. While I was raging inside, the advice came calmly:
monitoring, diet education. My self-image was crumbling
into pieces like some giant crack in an ice shelf,
a failed health self. But time heals, the rough edges
get smoothed over, second opinions take the heat out,
your better self emerges, all is not lost. Like a tired
labrador, I am grateful for the gentle treatments.

[29 July 2017]

TURANGALILA
For Karl Texler

Derived from two Sanskrit words, translated as 'love song
and hymn of joy, time, movement, rhythm, life, and death',
so Olivier Messiaen called his symphony of love
ecstatic song calls never heard before,
recording the bird sounds on his forest walks
around La Mure, homeland of Father Eymard.
Simone Young marshalled one hundred musicians
in Hamer Hall saying the music was a 'nightscape'.
The truth is you are the composer, you are
the orchestra and you are the conductor,
rehearsing each night the silent music
of your unique cries of the heart
powered by holy longing, purified by human tears.
One still night the hyper drive of your soul will engage
and you will sail to Eliseum carried in the arms
of your personal angel to meet your God.

[30 July 2017]

THE SUGAR DRAGON

Referred to a public hospital – 'Are you an in-patient?'
'No!' 'I'm sorry'. But got a mid-city clinic name and was told
'we don't do that anymore' and got a person this time, who said,
'I'm on maternity leave, but my colleague might be able to help.'
So met with the nurse the next day and told there was
little wriggle room as I was not overweight and the diet was
not too bad. The mysteries of the chek-er were explained,
how it gets and reads your blood. 'Now you do it tonight
and in the morning'. Amazingly the levels come down,
I am on the way. Not so fast, my blood won't come,
thus no results. I'm going nowhere. Finally a decision
is made – hospital – so I can be thoroughly reviewed.
I' m rolled into my room, sharing shower and toilet.
Have only the basics with me. The battery of tests
and monitoring begins done by team of nurses,
specialists, pharmacists and health professionals.
All my health anomalies are exposed one by one;
No hiding places. But with this emerges my true
situation and the hope of effective treatment.
Home again, the fearsome giant gestalt has resized
into a little bulldog who trots along with me on daily walks.
[1 September 2017]

MOUNTAIN

Grand, majestic horizons of peaks, towers,
faces, walls and summits of dry rock, icy pinnacles
and avalanche prone snow. Not human terrain,
but there they are, tiny and insignificant.
Mountains of the Mind, Robert Macfarlane says,
'keep us in wonder and free from arrogance.'
The amazing spider-man Alex Honnold
free soloed El Capitan in four hours.
There is terror, exultation, despair, falls and death.
They climb, stamp up fragile ice cliffs,
para-ski down vertical snow slopes without end,
bike along razor ridges, and queue up on Everest.
These athletes dance up the steeps
in a way that those who are deaf to sound cannot
grasp. All this set to music by Richard Tognetti,
Vivaldi and Beethoven, performed
by the Australian Chamber Orchestra,
an outstanding film at the MIFF 2017.

[13 August 2017]

MONSTER BOMB

Monster bomb uncovered on Frankfurt campus.
All residents asked to evacuate in a three km radius.
My cousin lives right on the edge of this; many times have
I stayed there, even walked down the street where the bomb lay.
Ironic that this monster slept there only 350 metres from
the US military and later NATO HQ. Mum worked there
as a secretary to a US army captain. I even peeked
into the Eisenhower room which is now a museum
after the collapse of the Berlin Wall and communism.
The bomb was defused, how many more are undetected?
Life goes on in the city and the Goethe University named
after its Renaissance scholar, writer and administrator.

[4 September 2017]

DISPELLING THE DIABOLIC
For Peter Murnane OP

Bishop Geoff Robinson warned the Church
of caste, class and displays of priests versus people
in those called to be servants, the least of all.
Reclaim the compassionate spirit of Jesus,
birth hierarchs of holiness, not power!
The Messiah came to serve, not to be served;
his 'bodiment shows the unity of sacred and secular,
it's not about preserving privileges. *All comes from God
and will return*, so Julian of Norwich. As we approach
ninety years of service at St Francis, let us dispel
the diabolic cleft of caste, for Christ united flesh and spirit,
giving us his body and blood, double helix word and symbol:
Take and eat, take and drink, all of you.
Letting go status and rank - what a centenary
there might be in 2029 if we were a truly servant
community bringing God's people fully on board!
For Jesus did not shun the sick, sinners, poor, unclean,
and outsiders, welcoming everyone into the kingdom.
*When privilege, power and dominance are more evident
than love, humility and servant-hood in the church,*

then the very Gospel of the servant Jesus is at risk,
says Bishop Vincent Long OFM Cap.

[28 September 2017]

PAULINE MUSIC

Habakkuk the prophet sang in half a sentence
the upright will live by faith energising
Paul to compose sonatas, concertos
and symphonies of faith. *All have sinned,
Jew and Gentile* alike need God's grace;
which enacted breeds *Zadoks*.
Faith is such a slippery word, almost audio
invisible, not crashing, clashing on the hammer
of our inner ear; it's bread and butter stuff
wrapped in a hifalutin word. Would we had
strong speech like German *Glaube,* Scandi *Tro*
or Gaelic *Chreideamh!* Not a heady word is faith,
nor a ghost in a machine, but full bodied
and blooded, a winged word, which seizes
eagle-like our humdrummery and raises us up
into transcendence and godliness.

[22 October 2017]

THE FREE GIFT

Too good to be true? We are on guard
for the fine print, the unticked box, the never-ending
list of conditions. This is not a "double Irish"
tax scheme, an accountancy trick to avoid tax
by becoming a tax haven. No, this is about eternal life,
about really accessing heaven; this is no junk freebie;
not 'where's the catch?, not 'too good to be true'.
Gift with no strings attached, no tit for tat,
joyously given, no reciprocity, no covenant
of equal rights, totally beholden to you Lord.

[24 October 2017]

BIKEFIXTATION

At Willesmere Park, on the Yarra Trail,
totem tall in stainless steel, pillar straight
crowned with tools, octopus arms cabled
with spanners, screwdrivers and gadgets
post tethered, refuge of riders, caught on the hop,
even offering air pressure service!
The only thing I didn't have was a bike,
I was on foot! No need to carry the leather
pouch with the basics under the saddle seat.

[25 October 2017]

THE AVOCADO TREE

Mighty Avocado, chief of trees,
self-pollinating dark green giant
planted by Br Vincent as a seed
marking time until Melbourne
Central provided the frostless
climate and windless shelter,
now contender for tree of paradise,
three storey tall in our city garden,
crowned with abundant fruit,
that only nimble students can
collect with high harvesting poles.

[27 October 2017]

BRUSH WITH A BURRA

Ideal walking day, not too hot, sunny but gentle breeze
to cool down the Warrandyte Goldfields trampers
pausing at the Pound Bend tunnel built to by-pass
the Yarra for fossicking with the water surging
after the recent rains retreating to the wooden bench
and table in the shade, unpacking the lunch box,
chomping into the grainy bread, avocado and chicken
when woosh, feathers brush my right cheek and
the fillings are gone and I stare amazed
at the cheeky kookaburra checking out his catch,
gazing wistfully at the sign on the wooden table,
'Don't feed the birds, keep the wildlife free'.
But what if they help themselves?
Stephen Spender envied Robert Lowell
his gritty, gristy gift of calling up the playdough
of life and death, forming it into art:
the '*wildest things eat out of your hand*'.

[9 December 2017]

HOW BEAUTIFUL THE FEET

What sound do the feet make? I mean the gospel feet
bringing good news not the marching and thudding of boots
hitting the road in thunderous unison; more the dance,
more the tinkle of the scallop shell on the backpack;
more the slosh of water in the drinking bottle.
How beautiful are the feet of those who bring good news!
A joyous noise, happy and expectant,
as a brook nourished by spring rains rills and trills
along its winding course, like the two foot wide
Goulburn at Woods Point where you scoop up a trout
with one hand.

[9 December 2017]

FAMILY SHIELD[11]
For Brett Crisafulli

There is no family coat of arms or escutcheon,
I invented a crest to honour my four grandparents:
on my father's side from Dortmund,
are Hugo Dirks and Toni Henneberg,
who I never knew; from northern Bavaria
on mother's side, Josef Roser and Franzi Kern,
with whom I lived for 7 years. They were not nobles,
any of them or titled gentry, no *von, zu, Graf* or *Herr*
among them, but commoners, ordinary folks.
My vain folly exists in chosen wood, bronze and paint,
having no past and no future. It is a device
my mind has made, a shield which I enjoy:
dexter chief, noble half eagle and *sinister* chief,
two roses, *dexter base*, a humble fowl, and *sinister*,
a crescent moon. Emblems impaled, marshalled
together, bearing my life motto, *Virtute non vi*,
the classic four: control, care, courage and fair go

---

[13] The shield was designed by a heraldic expert from my instructions. My uncle Walter Dirks was an inspirational figure for me. Because of his writings against Hitler he was silenced by the Nazis with the threat of the concentration camp. After the war he flourished as a writer and publisher with focus on the moral and political landscape of Germany. He has received many national and civic honours. See also my poem Meeting of the Cousins.

and the divine trio: trust, dream and passion.
I bear their joint DNA aging fast.

[28 December 2017]

MEETING OF THE COUSINS
To Gaby Dallwitz

First cousin Gaby and I got out of the U Bahn
at Ostendstrasse, walked along the Eschenheimer
   Anlage past the locked Russian Consulate
   to the multi storey Haus der Volksarbeit
   to honour Uncle Walter's role 70 years ago
   when a few civic believers met in the ruins
     of Goethe's bombed out ruined city
to chart a way forward for future politics.
Inside the *Walter-Dirks-Saal*, Gaby whispered
'I think Walter's two daughters are over there".
I looked across and added, 'Yes, but there are
   two more as well!' The Walter-Dirks-Tag
   in Frankfurt drew Walter's four daughters,
my second cousins. Clara and Elisabeth I had met
in Köln and Colmar but not Maria and Teresia.
   A happy meeting over *Wein* and *Pretzels*,
five homing pigeons plus a wide winged albatross
   from the ends of the earth down under.
     Oh! Dream of joy! Is this indeed
     The light-house top I see?

Is this the hill? Is this the kirk?
Is this mine own countree?[14]

[20 December 2017]

---

[14] The final four lines are from The Rime of the Ancient Mariner by S. T. Coleridge.

KUSINETREFFEN
To Gaby Dallwitz

Erste Kusine Gaby und ich sind raus der U Bahn
an Ostendstrasse, gingen die Eschenheimer
Anlage entlang, das russische Konsulat vorbei
zum kleinen Hochhaus der Volksarbeit
Onkel Walter zu ehren, der schon seit siebzig Jahre
in einen kleinen Gruppe in Goethes ausgebombte,
ruinierte Stadt die politische Zukunft vorbereitet.
Von drinnen der Walter-Dirks-Saal, Gaby flüsterte,
'Ich glaube die Töchter von Walter Dirks sind da'.
Ich blickte rechts und fügte hinzu, 'Jawohl, richtig
aber da sind noch zwei mehr'. Der Walter-Dirks-Tag
in Frankfurt hatte die vier Töchter hingezogen,
meine zwei Kusine Clara and Elisabeth
hatte ich in Köln und Colmar getroffen,
nicht aber Maria und Teresia. Ein glückliches
Treffen mit Wein und Pretzel, fünf Heimtaube
und ein geflügelte Albatros von Erde-ende:
O Freudentraum! Hab wirklich ich
die Spitze des Leuchtturms erkannt?
Ist das der Hügel? das die Kirche?
das mein Heimatland?
[22 December 2017]

TRUE NARRATIVE

90th Anniversary of the SSS Arrival
To Pam and John Crack

Archbishop Mannix invited the SSS to Melbourne.
Eight came from the USA, by the *Chicago,*
Burlington and Quincy Railroad train,
steamer *Sonoma*, via Hawaii and Samoa,
brothers and priests, first to Sydney, into
the Spirit at Albury, terminated at Spencer Street,
then St Francis - a long, long way from home,
like the bells that Goold brought from Dublin
so they could ring, chime, peal, knell, toll and clang,
gospel tones to *Australia Felix* burghers;
sadly no merry tintinnabulation here,
bells being grounded outside the sacristy
frail church structure not weight bearing enough,
said the engineers. But the French-Canadian five,
Lachance, Thibault, Chalifoux, Saint Laurent,
and Gingras, the Italian Foghino, and two
New York Americans, Vey and Sullivan,
kept vigil before the Lord in the sacrament,
day and night in perpetual adoration.
The pre gold-rush church, once surprised at being

ennobled to cathedral status, now intravenous-ed
started a new ICU service at the age of 90!
The vocations came: Len, Pat, Jim, Bruce, Wilfred,
Elijah's cloak becoming the adorer's surplice,
priest house morphed to cloister; Yarra flats
to seminary, missions to Colombo and Bombay,
Founder canonized, one miracle in Caulfield.
Ninety years is not a century, but it is not
seventy five years either and worth celebrating!

[1 March 2018]

BLUE CAMINO

For Kerry and Jan Maher

Classic walking route to *Sántiágo catedral;*
camíno fránces, to meet Saint James; or out
to New Norcia Abbey where Salvado awaits;
or to Caroline Chisholm Cottage in East Maitland;
p'raps to North Sydney, Mary MacKillop's tomb;
or the Asian journey of Dr Glowrey
trailing from Birregurra to Bangalore;
Glowrey House, Catholic Women's HQ,
Fitzroy, named after this Servant of God.
A new opportunity rises - slake your pilgrim thirst
with *Way of the Magi,* Orion's belt contains
the three stars known as *Los Tres Reyes Magos,*
the three Wise Men, guiding the way
from Emu Plains, Glenbrook, Springwood, Lawson,
Wentworth Falls, Blackheath, Mt Victoria
to Bell hamlet, not by electric train, but by foot
on dirt tracks and misty views at each Epiphany.
Your patrons are Finbar, Aquinas, Mary
as mother, Canice, Xavier and merciful Jesus,
and the hosts welcoming the pilgrims at dusk.

[4 March 2018]

RUSSIAN MELODY

Climbing into a high wheel black beast
loaded with food and sleeping bags
bound for the Snowy with an overnight
at Bairnsdale to pick up our third pilgrim,
Ray, still mourning his Lithuanian wife,
with victuals enough to feed an army.
Stopping at Cann River for a welcome snack,
then off again across the border to Bombala
for lunch, then heading for the turn off
from the Snowy River Highway.
Jolt, bump and jump sonata, then
out of the bush appears the orthodox
double foot rest cross, car park,
multi-belled tower and watchdog.
A bearded monk meets and briefs us
re the morrow. We admire the icons that cover
all the walls and ceiling of the church.
Chockful hostel; this year the Gregorian
and Julian dates share Easter.
We three are lucky, six bed bunkroom

for ourselves. We rise in the dark at 5.30,
take the wrong track, then arrive in time
for morning prayer, candles only, office sung in parts.
The abbot potter welcomes us, the icon painter
presides at the Eucharistic liturgy, twirling
artfully the candelabra wheel, setting ablaze
the heavens we will see one day.
The faithful slip in, to be incensed
and blessed by the flowered cross.
The darkness flees in the morning light
as the icons come to life and colour;
Haunted and hallowed by the repeated Russian
melody with English words, *Christ is risen!*

[18 January 2018]

IRENE THE MARTYR[13]

For Bernadette McCormack

Irene I did not know you, only your sister.
You threatened to be sainted before the mother
founder Mary MacKillop herself.
Martyrs go straight to the express lane.
Footy loving, tennis playing, sportified
you said yes to the great outdoors of the Andes
highlands to work among the poor,
brave beyond duty, now immortalized
in the school that bears your name
where you dance in a glass icon, resurrected
Irene, head inverted, to heroicize young hearts
birthing them anew. We prayed for you,
at Como; now pray for us, oh matchless maid.

[25 February 2018]

---

[15] Irene McCormack (1938-1991) was a Sister of St Joseph. She was shot and killed by a Maoist group in Huasahuasi, Peru. The glass icon was designed by Perth artist Rose Reilly for the Irene McCormack College, Butler WA.

THE NEW SWIFT[14]

Not Lilliput, Brobdingnag, nor Houyhnhnm,
does the new Gulliver, *Snowman*, visit,
but the waterless flood of genetic tinker gone mad.
A brainy teen plays *Extinctathon* in the ruin
of what was, before enrolling at *Crick-Watson* Tech.
A female Swift mocks the foibles and fantasies
which fascinate, freeze and devour: *rakunk*,
cute cross of skunk and racoon, *wolvog*,
scary blend of dog & wolf, *spoat/gider*,
bullet-proof spider milk silk, happi-cuppa
and gen-chicken franchises bleeding trade wars
until hostile viruses wipe out humans,
and the yahoos left are laughable simpletons,
spliced genes turn mating organs blue.

[15 March 2018]

---

[16] Dr Jonathan Swift was the Dean of St Patrick's Cathedral, Dublin, and author of Gullivers' Travels. W. B. Yeats poetically translated the Latin epitaph composed by Swift for his tomb:
        Swift has sailed into his rest;   Imitate him if you dare,
        Savage indignation there   World-besotted traveller; he
        Cannot lacerate his breast.   Served human liberty.
Margaret Atwood is the author of the MaddAddam Trilogy; Oryx and Crake (2003), The Year of The Flood (2009) and MaddAddam (2013).

UNFINISHED ALPHABET

Atwood's waterless flood; Blake's *fearful symmetry*
Coleridge's ancient mariner; Donne's *send
not to know For whom the bell tolls;*
pilgrim Eliot in the waste land;
Frost's lesser road taken;
Goethe's Faust kampfing with time;
Hopkins' windhovering falcon;
John of the Cross's *sounding solitude;* Lowell's whale
death-thrash song; Murray's glorious divine sprawl;
Newman's *'Go forth, Christian soul, from this world'*[17];
Noonuccal's *displaced person in your own country;*
Patterson's *thumb nail dipped in tar;*
Rilke's cage padding panther;
Shakespeare's thought-act frozen Hamlet twist;
Thomas' *Do not go gently into that night;*
Whitman's lament *O Captain! my Captain!*[18]
Yeats's ladder starting and ending
in the foul rag and bone shop of the heart.

[29 March 2018]

---

[17] The Dream of Gerontius written by John Henry Newman was set to music by Edward Elgar.
[18] Written in 1865 after the assassination of Abraham Lincoln

WAY OF THE CROSS
For Peter Gador-Whyte

We poem the striking hued tapestry of snapshots
sewn by Sister Verna of Jesus' last town walk;
book-ended by the Taizé chants *ubi caritas*
and *Jesus remember me*; cool and sunny day,
large crowd, shops closed, paparazzi abound;
all ages – blesseds and woebegones, pilgrims and teary,
sinners and saints, strollers and wheelchairs;
three vans, two for sound, the third for
water bottles - toddlers and seniors,
sticks, wheelie walkers, telescopic poles
straw hats, baseball caps, some reversed,
T shirts, jackets and cardigans a'plenty;
Boots, trekkers, thongs and sandals;
languages, not just English, but Welsh,
Chinese and German; car park with cheap rate,
being a public holiday, police on bikes,
tram officials, marshals, the walrus
moustachioed brass helmeted fireman
waiting near parliament station for funds;
the aged architect still making the trek;

polyphony at St Peter's, Eastern Hill;
lay leaders at St Patrick's; small greenwood
cross midway tween cathedral spires
and Trinity Lutheran bluestone, is dwarfed
by four giant cranes vertical in the sky over
the ghosted masonic temple; clergy in suits, robes
and mufti; black hatted Archbishop joins
walk along Collins Street; where the ninth station,
Jesus crucified, is placed at 4.00 am
that very morning and is now blessed; drum beat
down the hill and through the cobbled arcade;
prammed twins Gabe and Gael fast asleep.
Did you spy the green Amazon parrot perched
on the young Asian's shoulder outside St Paul's?
Thus distracted we hear the invitation to assemble
at dawn on Sunday for the resurrection.

[31 March 2018]

THE CROSSING

For Marea Richardson

Glorious autumn sunny day; my footy team winning
after a shaky start against Carlton. Eucharist
at Mornington; Gerry O'Collins farewelled his brother
placing the ashes in the parish columbarium.
Via the freeway for 11 am ferry to Queenscliff;
parked opposite the police station, walked down the path;
seniors' return; picked up hot chocolate watching
the big craft berth and lower ramp to road.
Top deck is best; the red ensign straight in the breeze;
radar swivelling non-stop; long-boat derrick slung,
16 person rafts equal 200 souls, orange life buoys; past Portsea
wealth pads; no dolphins today, those messengers of joy;
sister ferry passes 200 meters away; three lighthouses
emerge, two white, one black; cars off first;
then us foot-folk, two subdued Jack Russells;
steam whistle loco welcome, is it the *Blues Train*?
Sighted the red brick Queenscliff Hotel; *Athelstane House,*
'small hotel by the sea' startles. Ringwood agape memories;
Noel's generosities: gifting new caps, shirts and DVDs.
How many times did Jesus cross the lake, day and night

with his disciples learning the new art of folk fishing?
Resting at a garden café with cheeky sparrows; met Lizzie
at double labyrinth *Santa Casa* for a June retreat preview,
absorbing worship spaces with Bass Strait sunsets
whilst lamenting retirement of loved Fr Richardson.
Resolved to see him, but he was at Barwon Heads
for a wedding; visited St George's atop the town,
and the memorial to the drowned crew of boat
George Tobin which foundered in 1991 storm,
the white/red pilot lights mounted on the church tower,
southern cross beacon of hope; inside a plaque
to Lieut. Edward Henry Richardson, Somme 1918.
At Swan Bay, 'Thomas the Tank engine' chuffed by
with the fat controller waving to the children.
Giant green 'Henry' stile-stairs in place,
parked invitingly. Passed the town bell, only to be rung
in the event of shipwreck. Dolphins elsewhere.

[8 April 2018]

BEYOND DEATH

For Colin Goodwin

Some have gone across the border into
the unknown land and come back. They speak
of bliss and joy, but they are not believed.
Proof, give us proof. Kerry Packer said
there's nothing there, not his field. Brain surgeon
Eben was dead for one week but came back
at a mortality and morbidity session. Ironic.

[22 April 2018]

BROKEN BRIDGE

The boy got out of the green bus one stop early
walked past the Tower Hotel to the grassy flats
where the four foot bridge spanned the Darebin creek
then up the steep track to the Fairy Hills
and the Napier Waller house and studio, not
knowing either, just homeward bound.
Now seventy years later he walks the new
broad ten foot path, signposted, line-marked,
flood boom, solar powered, fenced and netted,
yearning for the old bridge, finding it again
reduced to a stump; the bluestone spoon drain
is intact, too hidden and humble to be noticed.

[22 April 2018]

CHRIST'S FIREBRAND

Humour in the scriptures? Let me focus on
Christ's famous arsonist. At Athens Paul saw
his chance to impress. In fact he was nicknamed
a 'chattering magpie', says the NAB, but scored
an invite to the Areopagus. 'Before Paul could open
his mouth' the Roman officer Gallio told the Jews
he would watch them, but not act on their antics,
quibbles and fiddlesticks. That did not happen often,
he wasn't called Mercury for nothing, the honey tongued
messenger Hermes was the spokesman for the gods!

[13 May 2018]

THE PRODIGAL'S HUT[17]
For Galen Catholic College Wangaratta

Brand new story of a wild rural boy
and how he met his sheep hut end.
JC flees into wilderness, fearful of being
prime suspect of his drunken father's death.
Shepherd of the mist Fintan lives remote,
true to his core identity, this shepherd
becomes the sacrifice, providing the way
for Jaxie's future, even enabling his transport.
Jesus told this story long ago in a parable
and gave his life for our ennoblement.
We *take and eat* and become what we receive.

[5 June 2018]

---

[19] The poem was occasioned by a homily given to the staff and students of Galen Catholic College, Wangaratta with reference to Tim Winton's newly published The Shepherd's Hut.

THE POWER OF LOVE[18]

Many are the couples I have addressed
at their nuptials. Each is Harry, each is Meghan
eyes full of love as the great day arrives
never to be repeated, but lived out
with all one's mind, strength and heart.
Good Bishop Curry hymns the power
of love. Made by love, we were, meant
for love we were; no other way, no other
God, but alas we're clever in making
idols, ersatz loves; loves that don't heal,
don't set free; yes, the revolution of all
time is God's unconditional love of the world,
which Jesus made a template for us,
the game changer, the world changer,
the life changer. OK, you're not Peter,
you're not Paul, so what? You can love.

[6 June 2018]

---

[20] Bishop Michael Curry delivered the sermon during the wedding ceremony of Britain's Prince Harry, Duke of Sussex and US actress Meghan Markle in St George's Chapel, Windsor Castle.

REVISITING HARRY POTTER
For Anthony Nguyen

Sacrifice is an old word from another time
   but it surfaces again in Harry Potter,
the boy who survived a death curse, with just
a forehead scar, a memory he must interpret.
   Harry is no scapegoat, he endures, thanks
      to his mother's love and sacrifice.
   Read Balthasar's *Herrlichkeit* entire
in original language at Sankt Georgen
over Christmas 1998-99 and his great
conspectus of salvation in *Theodramatik*.
   poetic and imaginative literary works
     of saving grace in human hearts:
*creation of … finite freedom by infinite freedom
is the starting point of all theo-drama.*
   Does it take creative fiction to expand
   our grasp of what God achieved in Christ?
Deathly Hallows appeared in hardback
on all the supermarket shelves in Frankfurt.
   My sister says Harry taught her children
to read. Dumbledore – stumbling but wanting;

Snape – ambiguity supreme; Riddle in name
and nature, but bad, very bad; horcruxes,
death curses, need to be found and defused
just as life's toxic memories need healing;
Harry is the *Green Henry* of English prose,
maybe even the teenage *Young Werther*[21]
taking his own life, which Goethe and Harry didn't.
Sacrifice is a game of musical chairs, pass the parcel,
hot potato, cat and mouse, in seven volumes.
Harry survives, just. Life, like art, can be fun,
but high stakes, costing not less than everything.

[11 June 2018]

---

[21] The Sorrows of Young Werther, published in 1774, recounts an unhappy romantic infatuation that ends in suicide. Goethe admitted that he "shot his hero to save himself": a reference to Goethe's own near-suicidal obsession with a young woman during this period, an obsession he quelled through the writing process.

SEA BIRTH

Santa Casa Retreat, Queenscliff

Piloted safely through this narrow passage
englishless on the '*SS Orion*' with mother
starting new life at the world's bottom
with one suitcase in the year the steamer
'*Time*' was wrecked at land's end, Corsair Rock,
blown up for the doomsday '*On the Beach*',
sunk Good Friday 1960. Lived a' teen
off old Nepean Road, heard your whisper,
learnt Mornington cliffs and pier,
stumbled asleep as young chaplain
to befogged Easter dawn service,
migrant-chartered '*Ellinis*' sailing in circles.
Twice I passed over on '*The Spirit*'
to the Apple Isle for holidays,
crossing the Heads with my cousin
from Europe, now be thanked for my brothers,
Lord, master mariner of watery wildness.

[1 July 2018]

VERNACULAR CATHEDRAL
Confreres at St Francis

Pre-gold rush poor, dirt floored, no steps,
beloved by the Irish, chosen by McDonalds
and MacKillops for their wedding; Maria
   Helena baptized as their first born.
   Still there, post Goold art collection,
   gum trees gone, hewn into cathedra,
   'Why would you want three? phrasing
   Little Sister Simone, speaking of shoes
in the spirit of Francis and de Foucauld.
   Head office wanted to sell you off,
   even Ladye Chapel jewels, despatch
   New York migrants to a'Beckett St.
   The war saved you from demolition
      long before Heritage and Trust.
      Latin tones long silent, but
the vernacular, despite hopeful debut
   in '69, limps post 2010, looking
   for translation, scholars galore
   at Gerry O'Collins' talk on the
   ICEL Missal that never was.

House of prayer you are, earthy,
no wind bag Jeremiah *temple of the Lord*
people feeding from the common dish.

[29 July 2018]

CARNIVAL RIDE
For Philip Watkins

Wild ride with unknown GPS plugged in the dash
unseen voice clipping out precise commands;
today it is forty nine years since the oils were
given me and I said it seemed like yesterday.
Jinkered trucks roar past, no doubts for them,
as Schubert's *Death and the Maiden* brings sanity.
Wet 'n Wild flashes past, taking me back to a family holiday
on the Gold Coast. *Exit now*, M4 to M7, heaven help
the faint hearted. Bunnings pit-stop on the Richmond Road,
I do have a transponder after all, you just can't see it.
Whack – Riverstone truck kicks up a stone starring
the windscreen. *You have arrived at your destination*,
says the Tom Tom, as stone portal of BXVI appears,
open gates, thick bush, steep curves, creeks and floodways
before sharp rise to sports ground where
statues and tall castle church dominate.
Stop at not-chapel, but Cana dining hut
at kitchen; cook rings Chris who welcomes me
and gives grand tour: doubles, quad bunks, massive

five storey Church, two Bennies, abbot and pope.
Bush chapel best, table and log benches.
Flying fox needs un-gettable supervisor.
Switchbacks after Yarramundi crossing,
Dusk as I suss out service road access,
walking to the door of Briony and Jess,
dining at their family table, swapping stories
of the Shack, and the Bell Chapel to be
and the Blue Camino to come.

[4 August 2018]

TRUE GLORY

God is greater than the Temple
Ezekiel's vision of the temple, dream or real.
Holiness is formed in the woman
who said yes to God, growing in her;
not in the stylish hair-cut;
Henry Bucks wardrobe,
Armani jewelry, Lamborghini keyring,
Not in collar and cloak.
but the riders in the chariot are
battered mother, black queer artist,
greenie spinster, Shoah senior with the
German rainbow name, from White's palette.
Works, not words; Francis eyeballing the poor.

[27 August 2018]

I HAVE A DREAM
To Janiene Wilson

I have a dream that one day I will see
my companion from Nazareth inn
Holy Land retreat, Geoff Robinson -
*were not our hearts burning as
the hooded stranger walked with us -*
open a story telling, singing week
inside the Opera House sails.
There Pope Francis with a St Andrew
shepherd asking forgiveness
from Koories and abused alike
as the quay-tied barque of Peter,
impatient for the Spirit's breath,
to spinnaker its healing course
whilst upstream a donkey, waits
as waters roll over the new born
on the banks of the Snowy sketes.

[2 September 2018]

THE COLLEGE IN THE FIFTIES
For SPOCA

There is only ever one College: part Georgian, part bluestone,
coloured mosaic Loyola crest embedded in the stone floor.
Quig taking RE after lunch & talking about sex; we got
his compassion but not much else. Waking in the Watsonia night
as the dragon hissed and clanked to tame the retreat frost;
corridors evoking Elizabethan England and panels full
of hiding places; Lud reading Chaucer; Newton maestro
Fr William Moloney SJ teaching Leaving Physics at 80.
Footfalls echoing in the cathedral en route to a confessor;
the whole school perched on the eastern transept steps
for the annual photo; practising with our drum band
through the Fitzroy Gardens for St Patrick's Day March;
always Monsignor Fox presiding at the prize-giving,
but now beside Dr Mannix sitting in the saloon car taking
the salute at Parliament House, preaching at the yard
entrance to the crowds; confirming, inviting us to take
the pledge until twenty five; Tchaikovsky's *Peter
and the Wolf* at the Town Hall; concerts at Central Hall;
Barry Woods' superb delivery of Celtic folk songs;
Thorold Merrett's fiancée coaching us in make up

for the GS operetta. Assembly space for the rector's address,
Mass with the newly ordained Old Boys; and dance
lessons for the College Ball at the Victoria Hotel.
Sports Day at Victoria Park, moving from visitors'
to the actual CFC change rooms; doing of Huddy perhaps,
driver for honours awarded in Latin and French.
My new chum Adrian Conroy tops the handball comp
though three years younger; at the rifle range his skills
made him chief cadet marksman. Hearing the 'G roar
during the '56 Olympics as we dreamt through class,
sitting for public exams at the Showground; Denis Dalton
roving for the Pies in a premiership try one kick short;
the decade saw the Collingwood Magpies win two flags,
'gainst the Geelong Cats and Melbourne Demons;
rejoicing in *Giant* the movie marking end of school;
seasick in a fishing boat rocking off Werribee coast
with Hosking's small group; more fun in Sherbrooke
Forest on a similar outing. Doorknocking for the Cup
raffle to help the missions in India. Once and forever
a *Semper et ubique Fidelis* Patrician.

[16 October 2018]

NAMING OF BONNIE DOON
To Tony and Joan Tehan

John Bon – good in name, good in deed,
protector of the Taungurong, not by parliament
palaver talk, but welcoming blacks back to the
land, where they were born and learnt the lore
of their ancestors, five hundred camping
at Wappan, non-stop corroboree contra Benalla
massacre reprisals. Anne Bon, friending William Barak,
both with dead children, fighting for Corranderk wattle
and Yarra manna gums against the Ahabs,
finally campaigning for the Doon name change
so we joyfully sing: *We're going to Bonnie Doon.*
For there we spent our summer holidays
in the shadow of Mt Buller, fishing in the trout streams,
piloting on Eildon pond and swimming in its waters.

[8 November 2018]

BAPTISM OF THE TWINS
To Julian and Vicki Hamilton

Forty nine years ago, the young student priest comes
from the bell-bird banks of Lower Templestowe to pour
baptismal water on the heads of twins Paul Vincent
and Mark Phillip at St Bede's, North Balwyn[22].
Now the same blessing hand nears a Golden Jubilee
naming, anointing and christening twins Mark Timothy
and Sean Leo at St Mary's, East Malvern, speaking
the same words. The four evangelists gaze down
from the giant south window. But the world has moved:
Nixon morphs into Trump, Khrushchev to Putin; Gorton
to Scomo, even the church re-forms: Paul to Francis, Knox
to Comensoli, and us, Huot to Barbosa, and the mission houses
of Colombo, Kandy, Bombay and Madras kerning
into new Provinces with St Peter Julian Eymard placed
on the universal calendar of the Church on August 2.

[16 November 2018]

---

[22] Paul Vincent and Mark Phillip Soligo; father - Luciano Soligo; mother - Pamela Marshall 16 November 1969.

ELEGIAD

How can we sing the song of the Lord in an alien land?
Not twenty five hundred years ago but here and now.
Jesus saw the bent over woman in the synagogue. Not caring
it was the Sabbath, he was with her as was the synagogue
leader, full of *schadenfreude,* cold and indifferent; not so Jesus
filled with compassion he reached out and healed
her crippled spirit. Jesus did not judge or condemn her.
The leader rebuked the healed one: *Come some other day
and not on the sabbath!* Jesus stepped in with righteous anger:
You hypocrites! You untie your animals to water them.
Here is a daughter of Abraham unbound after 18 years.
Jesus imposed no penance, no conditions. Luke alone
tells this story, but Jesus always champions the poor
and broken, challenging the prideful arrogance of the elite.
The people rejoiced and sang a song of joy.

[3 November 2018]

SASHA THE BALLERINA

Spends all day in church, muttering soft,
loud, angry, potty mouth, verbal *dans macabre,*
entering during common morning
prayer wearing trademark ballerina
tutu and tights, despite the big frame,
miming the lyrebird with self-talk and counsel,
then comes the high pitched silly giggle,
triggering the angry parent gush of rebukes,
screams and expletives, some show! Suddenly,
you are the Pharisee delighting in your virtues,
thanking God you are not Sasha, until you
remember the parable Jesus told:
Lord, be merciful to me a sinner!

[26 November 2018]

FRANK IS NINETY
To Frank O'Dea

Frank turned up for Sunday Mass at Park
Orchards with his Akubra and silky white
beard into a well sprung people ambush.
The data projector hollered a '*Happy 90th
Birthday Father Frank*' bouncing echo
of the homily he offers them. Fifteen
young servers, mustered from *God's School,*
kitted in their flowing smocks, joyfully
jump sing an action song, springing for Frank,
an exuberant 360° rotation leap. Grand
finale - two light cream sponges and
a Western Bulldogs jumper, numbered nine
and zero. What a *Deo Gratias!*

[2 December 2018]

HARING 101[21]

For Greg Burke

Seven years a professor before donning
the uniform of Hitler's army he mapped
out *The Law of Christ,* the revolution
that replaced the harsh inquisitor
with the merciful Saviour, standing up
to the bullies and the SS, choosing
the medic path of Angelo Roncalli, rubbing
shoulders with the wounded, the sick,
whatever their speech; beginning in France
reaching out to civilians, paradigm
for his time on the Russian front; known as
'the doctor' beseeched to deliver a child,
when the midwife gave up. Neither
chaplain, nor officer, with no authority
to say Mass, he got round the rules.
Somehow led out three hundred battered
from the Stalingrad trap; Russian folk
taught him if you don't share your
bread with the hungry, how can you

---

[23] Bernard Haring, Embattled Witness: Memories of a Time of War, Burns Oats, London 1977

approach the table of the Lord's supper?
As pastor of a Polish parish the people
enabled him to avoid capture by the Red
Army for Christ comes to heal, not judge.

[28 January 2019]

IRISH DANTE
For Joseph O'Callaghan

Could not spell or say his name O'Siadhail
('Sheel') but now how could I forget him
for playing bridge with wordsmith Eliot
trumping him to win the poetry kitty?
The Five Quintets[24], Swiftian modernity,
full of genius, brilliance and perversity!
But the wedded bliss of Bach and Anna
Magdalena, Browning and Elizabeth,
Chagall and Bella, Mahler and Alma,
Mozart and Constanza, Rubens and Helene.
Thank God we are sustained by love, not
brute will and power, why even the old fox
Goethe realised as much and tempered
his Faustian finale. So no surprise
that Bonhoeffer and Hannah Arendt
feature in paradise among the table
guests chosen to feast with Angelo
Roncalli, Jean Vanier and Said Nursi.

[21 March 2019]

---

[24] Published in 2018

THE PARADISE TREE

Enamelled tabernacle for pilgrims,
Egino you baked in vibrant colours
cloisonéed to enchant God's people,
capturing a rainbow gospel: behind
the Cana couple Miriam and Jesus stand,
water jars wine brimming; boy bearing
bread and fish for Jesus to bless, groups
resting on green grass; dreamy Mary
all ears, grumpy Martha carping;
Thomas' doubting fingers stunned
by the open side; Magdalen amazed;
Emmaus disciples, eyes enlarged.
Rich varied treasures to still our
yearning for the manna of life,
tree of paradise, divine fruit more
wondrous than we had dared to hope,
won by love that did not count the cost.

[20 February 2019]

GHOST WALK

To the Templestowe-nians[23]

Bell-birds still calling non stop
all day in gums along the billabong,
silver-voiced ... darlings of daytime,
and the old Yarra foot-bridge sways
as ever. Fifty years have come and gone
since the bishop prayed for Christ's
priesthood to descend in the five storied
chapel where surpliced choirs sang;
but the hundred metre cloister tunnel
even now runs east to west with the sun;
the aisled library where students swotted;
the oval where teams played cricket;
the tennis courts of doubled shouts,
the cemetery emptied of its dead,
the bare grounds now fully treed and
forested like some enchanted castle
from the corpus of the Brothers Grimm.

---

[25] Dedicated to all the students who studied at Christ the King College, Lower Plenty, which had the postal address of Lower Templestowe, shortened in popular speech to Templestowe. The College functioned from 1955-1969 as a seminary. It then became a retreat house until it re-opened as Odyssey House. St Kevin's refers to the parish of Templestowe, Victora.

Once were orchards, tomatoes, chooks,
dairy cows, pigs, cattle and guard dogs.
The Kelly classic seminary could have
been a YTU campus for overseas students,
or St Kevin's Catholic College, now
perdures as Odyssey House, Pope Francis'
field hospital, much needed alt. drug
rehab with Governor Linda Dessau
launching a new lodging wing
for clients' families and children.

[20 February 2019]

ABIGAIL

For Abigail

Abigail, *Father's joy,* I first met giving
hospitality to David and his troops
when pursued by Saul, making good
the insulting refusal of her husband:
Brute is his name and brutal he is.[26]
Perhaps royal court redaction, even so,
boldness nowhere repeated in the bible
lauding her wisdom and good looks.
When Nabal dies, David offers her
his hand in marriage and she accepts.
Meeting two is the fictionalized fury
New England love thwarted village
in *The Crucible,* re-told terror tale,
despite Salem spelling peace, now
drowned in the horror witchcraft trials.
Third time comes a real woman, beautiful
like her model; not Miller's drama queen,
a true Magdalen risen Christ searching,
wonderfully become divine joy bearer,

---

[26] 1 Samuel 25:25

co-creator of new life. David to Abigail:
Blessed be the Lord, the God of Israel,
who sent you to meet me today![27]

[28 February 2019]

---

[27] 1 Samuel 25:32

DAMIAN THE TRAIN LOVER

The carer said *Damian, move over so
someone else can sit.* Someone did.
Opposite us sat an old Chinese man.
My name is Damian, holding his long
white cane, w*hat's yours?* Jo, I said.
Where are you going? To get a footy poster.
*I'm going to Southern Cross to watch
the trains.* You have to go Flinders St
for the steam train. *Oh, I would like
to see that.* Steamrail runs a Sunday
trip now and then. Wide grin creases
the face of the inscrutable Oriental.

[14 March 2019]

LES AND VALERIE

For Les and Valerie

English head of the Teachers' College,
hearing of my wish for a group reading
of *The Boys who Stole the Funeral,*[28]
suggested I contact you. So I knocked on
your door and met you both. Les you kindly
offered to speak the indigenous voices,
which you did one night at Balmain Point.
Then in mid-summer by our grandest river
met once more at Mildura writers' festival.
Enthused I gave a talk on *Fredy Neptune*[29]
in our new Pastoral Centre. My flickering
poetic muse fell dormant in my thirties,
the flow was to proclaim, preach, sing
the Word. You came to Montsalvat,
where Matcham Skipper mentored me
in my student years crafting with wax,
for the launch of *The Biplane Houses*[30].
But after my Spanish walk, the gift awoke.

---

[28] Published in 1979
[29] Published in 1999
[30] Published in 1979

At Q/A Rabbi Boteach passionately spoke
of marital intimacy as the lot of human life.
May this love sustain you both and always.

[14 March 2019]

THE CHEMO STAR-RUCK[29]
For Graeme Duro

Westendplatz jolts you. I had played there as
an urchin, thrilled by the sled whooshing
to the dam's icy bottom. I stoop to look
down at the rough stone block on the grass,
monument to the deliverance of the frail, sick,
life threatened, Karen Blixen too, donor of
Babette's Feast, Out of Africa and more.
Medical messiah Paul Ehrlich lived nearby,
nobled for painstaking research, curing infections,
finding the new chemotherapy door to address
our invasive cancers. The sculpture invites you
to sit on the built-in seat twixt the bison horns
and female bust. Though the good doctor died in '15,
his widow had to flee from Hitler to a Swiss haven.
Opposite, the Jewish high school nears completion;
its police post already in place, waiting and ready

[18 June 2019]

---

[31] Paul Ehrlich was born in 1854 in Silesia, now part of Poland. He was awarded the Nobel Prize in Medicine in 1908 for his work in haematology, immunology, and antimicrobial chemotherapy. He is acknowledged to be the founder of chemotherapy. Westendplatz is a small park between the main railway station and the University. Erhlich died in 1915 and is buried in the Jewish section of Frankfurt Cemetery.

BURG ROTHENFELS

Red rock castle high above the river Main,
conspiring with the Spessart forest to hide
Burg Rothenfels with its distinctive squat
tower, bought from Count Löwenstein
in 1919 overlooks the small town below;
nursery of the Quickborn Youth movement,
with focus on young adult formation
100 years old (the castle dating from 1150);
strong symbols of gold cross and rising sun
on a blue field, both anti *Volk und Führer*,
where Romano Guardini was chaplain,
and Walter Dirks his enthusiastic scribe.
I toiled up the steep stone staircase from town to
summit, admiring the view, through the tunnel
crossing cobblestoned courtyard. The knights'
banquet hall used for conferences and weddings.
Rudolf Schwarz began his lifework in the Burg
chapel. Mary s head, saved from the Nazis,
then hidden, now graces the chapel. Mentor
Guardini is *en route* to sainthood, as teacher,

liturgist, writer, professor and author of *The Lord*.
I leafed through his library books and *Festschriften*
archives, savouring uncle Walter's memories.

[16 July 2019]

ICE 529 AT FRANKFURT HBF[30]
To John and Liz Wright-Smith

Vacation season, kindergartens, schools, unis
closed for family time, much travelling by plane,
autobahn, train; three murderous shoves
on platform 7 as the Düsseldorf train glides in
at 9.50 bound for Munich at 9.54, cancelled
by the track fall death of the 8 year old boy,
lucky 'scape of mother; 78 year old knocked
down, citizen arrest of an Eritrean refugee;
media awash with rumour, talkfests launched,
everyone in the street has a point of view.
Teen Thérèse of Lisieux prayed for the convicted
triple murderer Pranzini who, rejecting the priest
as the guillotine was readied, then on impulse
three times kissed the cross placed before him.
Tokyo gated platform barriers are proposed.
How can you insure for mistrust of the stranger?

---

[32] An ecumenical service was held by the Bahnhof Mission two days later 31 July in the forecourt of Frankfurt Railway Station. On-line donations, courtesy of Hessische Rundfunk, tallied €45,000 on 2 August 2019. The Caritas aged care facility Santa Teresa in the north western Frankfurt suburb of Hausen, was the place where the father-in-law of my cousin´s daughter lived for a month before his death.

Jesus gave us the parable of the Good Samaritan!
At Altenzentrum Santa Teresa the Eritrean priest
says Mass; on 1 August the Neviges pilgrim passed
by the massed teddy bears, candles and flowers.

[3 August 2019]

ICE 529 AM FRANKFURT HBF
Zu den Ungenannten Mutter

Ferien – Kitas, Schule, Unis – alle zu für Familien Zeit.
Viele reisen süd mit Flugzeug, Autobahn und Zug.
Drei mordvolle Stösse auf Gleis 7 als die weisse ICE
gleitet an am 9.50 für Abfahrt 9.54, annulliert von
tödlichen Schienenstürz des achtjährigen Knabes,
glückliches aber trauriges Überleben der Mutter,
auch eine acht und siebzige Person ist auf Steig gestossen,
ein Eritreer verhaftet von Passanten – Medien rasen
mit Gerüchte, Politiker machen endlose Talkshows;
jedermann hat seinen eigenen Blickpunkt.
Thérèse von Lisieux betete für die Seele der dreimal
Mörder Pranzini, der wollte gar nichts vom Priester.
Als die Guillotine hoch geht, der nicht-Franzose küsste
dreimal den Kreuz Christi vor seinen Augen. Tokyogleis
-trennwände sind uns vorgeschlagen. Aber wie kann
man sich versichern von Ausländer Misstrauen?
Jesus hat uns das Gleichnis von guten Samariter gegeben!
In Hausen Altenzentrum Santa Teresa der Priester aus Eritrea
betet die Eucharistie; am ersten August der Neviges Pilger
läuft die massenhaften Bärchen, Kerzen und Blumen vorbei.

[2 Auguat 2019]

NEVIGES PILGRIMAGE CHURCH

The giant big top soars above the small town
like a Lyonel Feininger painting come to life,
marching out of a museum, transforming
itself into a great solid concrete pyramidal cube
vast and silent. A pilgrim tent for a pilgrim people
hiding jewels – not just the Eucharist in its giant
rose monstrance in the crypt, not just the oldest
image of the Immaculate north of the Alps, but
the relics of the great Scottish philosopher,
thinker and promoter of the Immaculate,
the Franciscan who died in Cologne, John
Duns Scotus.[33] All thanks go to Cardinal Frings
who promoted the unknown young architect
Gottfried Böhm's exciting 1963 design giving
flesh to the Vatican II phrase, *the people of God.*

[2 August 2019]

---

[33] Scotus is buried in the Church of the Friars Minor, Kolpingplatz, Cologne. His tomb bears the Latin inscription: Scotia me genuit. Anglia me suscepit. Gallia me docuit. Colonia me tenet. (Scotland brought me forth. England sustained me. France taught me. Cologne holds me.)

LOOKING BACK
For Liam Gibbons

Fifty years of serving as a priest by bushwalking!
The young man rejoining his club on a commando
weekend, travelling light to the Wonnangatta River,
no fresh trout, freezing overnight, but breathless
at Mass after the hot climb up the steep valley.
With Frank tent massing to Australia's hard to reach
mountain, protected by an unbridged wild river,
a vertical spur, five peaks and there, the dark tower
of Federation Peak, escaping its awesome embrace
straining a hamstring after three days of rain and slush.
Then came the Camino spiritual exercises across
Spain to Santiago where St James the Apostle rests.
With confrere Ken twice to the double moated Castle,
no fear of ropes or exposure, standing on top in mist
turning 'the best one day walk in NSW' so Bob Carr,
into overnight drama thanks to my dehydrated state.
Finally, this July, almost summiting
my magic nine thousand Bavarian alp
with my nephew Liam, power to him.

[9 October 2019]

FORGIVENESS

Cheap grace, costly discipleship, so Bonhoeffer
in the Nazi era. Blockages stop life, so what do
we do? Nurse the wound? Carry the guilt of slaying
his brother, like the slaver Rodrigo Mendoza in the film
The Mission, up the Iguazu Falls, all his armour and
battle kit? No, we do what Jesus did and would do,
forgive from the heart, let go, let life flow to each
capillary, near and far, to each chamber, passageway
and corridor of the human heart, despite our Hitlers
of political correctness or Himmlers and Goebbels
bureaucrats and all their red tape and on-line dicta
notwithstanding.

[26 November 2019]

KRISTALLNACHT CANTATA[32]
For Anthony Halliday

Oh why this meeting of kindred spirits
united in love against a wave of racist
fury and scorn? Otto Jontof-Hutter, in
Dachau, the brave William Cooper, and
I who fit in late in the day of this drama,
born out of time, present at the premiere
of this great communion of heart and mind,
fated to play a minor role as one who stood
by helpless by as the great wrong was
done in our name. The German consul
who made good the refusal to receive
the protest in the name of the people,
though Martin Sasse backed the Nazis
with all his might. The twenty nine piece
Cantata pays tribute to this unique man
immortalized in music and song. May
his like be seen again when those who
thirst for justice raise their voice for
the truth in every place and time.

[9 December 2019]

---

[34] The Kristallnacht Cantata, composed by Aron Trigger, was given its world premiere at Temple Beth Israel, Melbourne on 8 December, 2019, under the baton of David Kram,

PRAYER FOR NORMA JEAN

Lord, receive this woman known by the world as Marilyn Monroe,
not her real name, which is known by You alone;
her father unknown, robbed of her childhood when
raped at the age of six of her innocence and youth
and at sixteen wanted to kill herself; she married
instead, to avoid returning to the orphanage. Dreamt of being
a movie star, she dyed her hair blonde;
got a contract with Twentieth Century-Fox and was noticed.
Bullied, she fought to be taken seriously as an actress despite
the theatre moghuls, directors and co-stars; after two failed
marriages, she turned to alcohol and tranquilizers to cope;
when found dead from a suspected overdose, the phone
call she had made repeated the message
on a voice recording: WRONG NUMBER.
Before Harvey Weinstein and the #METOO movement, she
sought her own way; psychiatrists interpreted her dreams,
her defender and advocate, the Nicaraguan revolutionary,
poet-priest, Ernesto Cardenal, died on 1 March 2020 aged 95.
The temple of her body veiled, her face devoid of make-up,
no press agent, make-up assistant, paparazzi in attendance,

she now has all the time in the world.
Lord,
You fulfilled all the yearnings of the Samaritan woman -
You answer that telephone!

[16 March 2020]

THE CEMETERY

Left behind on All Souls Day in an empty house,
with our almost centurion on a mild Spring day,
as the Community gathers at Williamstown to pray,
remember and recall our dead in this time of Covid.
There is Graeme Duro, *Big Blue*, a giant of a man,
gone before the pandemic, his Saints made the footy finals,
no mean feat; Willie Bracken, from *Stoush* Melbourne,
long bonded with *The Disciples* and the against the tides man,
Vincent Laurisen, the unflappable Queenslander,
forever glued to the weather channel, just missing
the election result, of Labor's victory, Pauline Hanson's
defeat and the rise of the Greens. I did not go
because I did not feel safe on the uneven ground
at our plot. I missed the drive, high over the West Gate
Bridge and the old cemetery opposite the Victorian Railway
Museum. I gaze out my window to the giant avocado tree
that soars upwards with its dense green canopy of leaves
and utter a prayer of thanks for the gift of life as the sun
shafts the city with its midafternoon rays,
my walker parked alongside the printer.

[2 November 2020]

THE VIDEO TECHNICIAN
To Fr Dang Le

The weekly task of recording digital images
meticulously, faithfully and artistically,
camera and tripod set up in the sanctuary,
framing the scene, organist, cantor, reader,
presider, distilled by you into electronic data,
later edited together in a mix of sound,
organ, voice and speech, a celebration,
a marriage of life that defied the Covid
lockdown, and uploaded to the global world
of the internet, where your craft broadcasts
the good news of God's love to all and sundry
making St Paul, the great communicator
of the Messiah who gave his life for us,
envious of your skill and prowess on U Tube.

[16 December 2020]

WEISBACH ROMANCE
To Jack and Hilde

Both catapulted together by circumstances
beyond their control; for Jack it was weeks
of flight in Greece, then Crete from the Krauts
and their superior arms, then capture, by steam train
through the Balkans, Austria to the centre of the Reich.
For Hilde, the journey was psychological,
not geographical; she had received the news of Hans' death
at Sebastopol in the Crimean peninsula.
She had an infant, me, to remind and console her.
The soldier who brought the news gave back
the photos of the radiant mother and happy babe.
Hans carried this keepsake in his chest pocket now
pierced by the bullet that killed him. My grandparents
told me that story on my first visit home & showed me.
I remember asking mum as a young teen about Brunnhilde
when 3LO broadcast *The Valkyrie*. I remember the kitchen
door in Florence Street next the stove where
so many exchanges took place. From the story,
I understood the passion in Hilde which burned within her.
She sang songs out loud in the house from pure joy and happiness

in German as she busied herself about the house.
She looked forward to meeting her Monash friend Gudrun,
daughter of the organist of the Kaiser Wilhelmskirche in Berlin
who held poetry readings in her Robin Boyd house at Eltham
and later Nunawading. This was when I heard Schillers
Glocke, the bell that sounds the ups and downs & tragedies
of life. The Weisbachers still relate the Romeo and Juliet
evening serenades between Hilde and Jack from cousin
Irmgard's house and the POW barn across the narrow street.
I remember a group of men encircling me as a messiah prince
giving me bread topped with berry jam before the war's end.

[24 February 2021]

TRUE CLANCY
Damien Cash

    A. B. ('Barty') Paterson, a Sydney legal scribbler,
not a bush bard, mailed an unknown Clancy aiming
to retrieve a debt in the far west at *'Overflow'* sheep run,
where Gunningbar Creek entered the Bogan River, read
of a huge cattle drive beyond the Queensland border.
In the fifties, schools made lawyers and public servants,
we mavericks learnt *Clancy of the Overflow* by heart,
the bush ballad sprung from 'Banjo's' verse in print.
    At campfires we sang lustily *Waltzing Matilda*,
not knowing Chrissie Macpherson wrote the music
which she gave to Banjo who penned the words.
    At Glenmaggie we saddled Jack Higgins' steeds
and rode along the river flats of the Macalister.
Bonnie Doon saw us north of the Great Dividing Range,
where Jack Lovick's mountain cattlemen under Mt Buller
clad in their oilskins, Akubras, whips and horses
were to ride for the film *The Man from Snowy River*.
I trod those peaks of the High Country - Kosciuszko,
Jagungal, Feathertop, Howitt, Jaithmathang and Bogong.
Jack Thompson who played Clancy, came to our church,

where the upcoming stockman was schooled, confirmed.[35]
Clancy made his will with 'Barty' in Sydney in 1899.
Asked the year before if he were Paterson's drover, said
'I am reputed to be the man', quoting from his poem:
> *Over arid plains extended*
> *My route has often tended,*
> *Droving cattle to the Darling,*
> *Or along the Warrego;*

After sixty years of droving, back came the overseer
to Port Philip, retired in Carlton, with astounding recall
of Fr. Geoghegan meeting the urchin gaming marbles,
glimpsing that spirit of adventure and daring him to
become an altar boy at St Francis; sold Fawkner's
Port Philip Patriot as a newsboy; saw a woman, two
men in the William Street stocks; serene with wife
Ellen and their children, Annie novice with the Sisters
of the Good Samaritan in Glebe. Four-nine-fourteen
was 'Clangerald' called to the last muster.

[24 September, 2021]

---

[35] Jack Thompson, the star of *The Man from Snowy River*, read in St Francis Church, Lonsdale Street, Melbourne, the poetry of C. J. Dennis and 'Banjo' Paterson on 1 December, 2009. The poems were recorded.

APPENDIX

NOTE ON THE HORNSBY WATER CLOCK

"This is the Hornsby Water Clock located in the centre of Florence Street pedestrian mall in Hornsby. Thanks to my good friends and ex-Hornsby locals @whothedickens for giving me their grand tour.

Titled "Man, Time and the Environment" the clock weighs approximately 20 tonnes and stands 8 meters tall. The sculpture was unveiled in 1993 and cost over $1m to build. The bronze, stainless steel and glass construction took 2.5 years to build.

It has three water powered clocks including a 4th century BC Greek clepsydra, an 11th century Chinese water wheel clock and a 17th century Swiss pendulum clock. It also has a 17-note bronze carillon which rings automatically on the hour. Though this can also be played manually. Mrs Dickens recalled her memory of a gentleman donning gumboots before striding through the water to the middle of the fountain to delight a crowd with a tune. The fountain sits on a floating pontoon that rotates as a standard analogue clock pointing to Roman numerals on the perimeter of the fntain.

According to a plaque nearby, the sculpture is intended as "a unique environmental statement, particular relevant to Hornsby, an area retaining extensive unspoilt natural areas with abundant land and marine based flora and fauna" as it represents native animals such as the tawny frogmout, little penguin and other lizards, birds and possums.

An interesting youtube clip (see sources) shows the mixed reaction to the clock at the time of its installation. Some people labelled it a monstrosity, others admired it, others were just confused. The clip also describes how for much of its early years the clock was not working. Chicken bones were to blame as they were discarded into the fountain they would interfere with the fountains filtration system.

It's understandable how something so unique would have caused a stir when it was first unveiled, especially given its large cost and prominent position at the centre of Hornsby's main mall. Note: I try to be as accurate as possible but make no guarantees. Please use this infrmtn at your own risk.

Sources: https://en.wikipedia.org/wiki/Hornsby_Water_Clock
https://youtu.be/RWtfsDK43-Q

Published March 5, 2016"

www.ingramcontent.com/pod-product-compliance
Lightning Source LLC
Chambersburg PA
CBHW072048290426
44110CB00014B/1602